The Original Benedict Option Guidebook:

Benedict of Nursia's Own Rules for Living Christian Community in a Post-Christian Society

The writings of St. Benedict newly translated and topically organized with commentary for practical application

by

Cameron M. Thompson, Psy.D, MA

Cameron M. Thompson

"All that is gold does not glitter,
Not all those who wander are lost.
The old that is strong does not wither,
Deep roots are not reached by the frost.

From the ashes a fire shall be woken,
A light from the shadows shall spring;
Renewed shall be blade that was broken,
The crownless again shall be king."

—J.R.R. Tolkien

Published by

Marchese di Carabàs

ISBN: 978-1-7356578-0-6

CONTENTS

PREFACE

When Rod Dreher published his book *The Benedict Option: A Strategy for Christians in a Post-Christian Nation* in 2017, he had already been speaking about the concept of the Benedict Option (or BenOp, for short) for a number of years. Dreher's original articulation of the Benedict Option took its inspiration not only from a 6th century holy monk from Nursia, Italy, but also in part from the highly influential work of Alasdair MacIntyre, *After Virtue*. Both MacIntyre and Dreher (and many others in between and since) have called out the fact that modern society in the secular global West is no longer conducive to the Christian way of life in any meaningful sense of the term—and that this has in fact been the case for quite some time. Dreher describes the essence of the Benedict Option as referring to "Christians in the contemporary West who cease to identify the continuation of civility and moral community with the maintenance of American empire, and who therefore are keen to *construct local forms of community as loci* of Christian resistance against what the empire represents."[1]

The key takeaway from MacIntyre can be summed up where he says, "What [Benedict and his monks] set themselves to achieve... was the construction of new forms of community within which the moral life could be sustained so that both morality and civility might survive the coming ages of barbarism and darkness. If my account of our moral condition is correct, we ought also to conclude that for some time now we too have reached that turning point. *What matters at this stage is the construction of local forms of community within which civility and the intellectual and moral life can be sustained through the new dark ages which are already upon us.* [...] This time however the barbarians are not waiting beyond the frontiers;

---

[1] Rod Dreher, 2015. "Benedict Option FAQ" on *The American Conservative*. (https://www.theamericanconservative.com/dreher/benedict-option-faq/)

1

they have already been governing us for quite some time. And it is our lack of consciousness of this that constitutes part of our predicament. We are waiting not for a Godot, but for another—doubtless very different—St Benedict."[2]

So how would we characterize just what this way of St. Benedict looks like? St. John Henry Newman poetically describes how "St. Benedict found the world, physical and social, in ruins, and his mission was to restore it in the way not of science, but of nature. It was a *restoration* rather than a visitation, correction or conversion… Silent men were observed about the country, or discovered in the forest, digging, clearing and building; and other silent men, not seen, were sitting in the cold cloister, tiring their eyes and keeping their attention on the [page], while they painfully copied and recopied the manuscripts which they had saved… by degrees the woody swamp became a hermitage, a religious house, a farm, an abbey, a village, a seminary, a school of learning and a city."[3]

OUR PRECARIOUS PREDICAMENT

The eminent anthropologist of Christian history, Christopher Dawson, rightly points out that Christianity is an all-embracing system, such that everything pertains to the presence of God and all aspects of human life and culture are called to be elevated to the divine life God has created us for. This truth shines forth very clearly in the writings of St. Benedict. Increasingly in competition with Christianity, as Dawson continues, the modern politico-socio-economic machine is by its very nature totalitarian, and this is why Christians find themselves faced not only with a society that is no longer conducive to Christian life, but one where it is increasingly difficult—often impossible—to live as a Christian at all while remaining embedded

---

[2] Alasdair MacIntyre. *After Virtue*. University of Notre Dame Press, 1981.

[3] John Henry Newman. *The Benedictine Essays: The Mission of Saint Benedict & The Benedictine* Schools. Edited by C. Thompson. Acropolis Scholars, 2019.

within these socio-economic structures of their very nature incompatible with living the Gospel.

Such then, is our predicament. The individual Christian cannot survive. Each person needs community or they will perish, at least spiritually. Many—maybe you experience this firsthand yourself—are already going through life in the continual agony of spiritually languishing, barely holding on to faith, let alone any semblance of participating in a lived Christian culture in regular practice in their day to day lives.

OUR CALL TO ACTION

Cultural memory is the life-source of a people—and of individual persons. MacIntyre points out that, by our very nature as human beings, you are able to know what you should do *only* if you first know intimately what story, or stories, you are a part of. This cultural memory, however, is not something like book knowledge or abstract awareness, but is fundamentally a lived experience—something in which you become an active participant—and as such can only be lived in concrete, tangible communities: communities of Christian practice. Moreover, such communities must themselves be rooted deeply in the Christian tradition; communities detached from the deep roots of authentic tradition simply will not weather the storm, for *only **deep roots** are not reached by the frost.*

I cannot emphasize enough the importance of this fact for those situations where active persecution and soft totalitarianism threaten to extinguish Christian life entirely. It is not a matter of "circling the wagons" to flee from persecution. It is a matter of rooting yourself in the stability of practicing Christian communities so that you have the strength of faith and lived relationship with Christ our God to remain faithful in daily life, and in the face of whatever may come. Without this embeddedness in communities of Christian praxis, your Christianity will simply not survive.

But this is not only about strengthening yourself to *live not by lies* and resist totalitarianism (whether hard or soft), but the simple fact that Christianity is by nature communitarian and ecclesial, not individualistic. The "Lone Ranger spiritual gunslinger for Jesus" fantasy is an ideal of the americanist religion, but it is certainly not a Christian one. The true Christian hero—the saint—is inseparable from the Christian community of which they are a part, a member of the greater Body of Christ.

And so, if you haven't yet picked up on it, let this be your call to action: go seek out and cultivate new forms of living, tangible, local Christian community. The Benedict Option was proposed by Rod Dreher as a strategy for Christians living in a post-Christian world, but that strategy has been around for over 1,500 years, and there are great models to follow and learn from, not least of all the original monk from 6th century central Italy, from whom the Benedict Option takes its name. This book you right now hold in your hands is the original guidebook (the OG, if you will) from Benedict himself, giving us timeless wisdom on how to live this out. Let us be bold and follow where Christ our Master is leading us and, following this way, we will come to the wellsprings of new and everlasting life.

FOREWORD

By
Giovanni Zennaro[4]

Why are we following the Benedict Option? Because we have lost the social habit of living in community. It seems to me that in the second half of the twentieth century the West completed the mental *bourgeoisification* process that began with the Industrial Revolution. The main aspiration of the single person and family—regardless of social class—has become self-fulfillment and individual well-being. We have lost the idea of a human community as the context in which the person is born and grows, suffers and rejoices, sharing with the other members the deeper aspects of his own life. Even Christians have not been immune to this phenomenon. Faith has been reduced to one of the many values we try to maintain, rather than being the unique experience that gives taste and meaning to everything in life. Today we can clearly see that a faith of this kind, a practice that does not really affect our lives, can only survive for a few generations.

We live in a secularized society, imbued with relativism. Its teachings are often opposed to those of Jesus and his Church. I think it will be increasingly important for us Christians to practice particular ways of life, similar to the way of life of the first Christian communities. We will need places where faith is visibly expressed in every action of the everyday life. I mean a kind of oasis of faith—certainly not devoid of all our human contradictions and weaknesses—in which one can continuously regenerate

---

[4] This foreword first appeared in an interview of Zennaro by Rod Dreher on the blog, *The American Conservative*, in 2019. (https://www.theamericanconservative.com/dreher/benedict-option-cascina-san-benedetto-family-monastery/).

oneself. This should also allow us to live better as true Christians in the world out there. "You are the salt of the earth, but if salt has lost its taste, how shall its saltiness be restored?" (Matthew 5:13): we need—at least I think I need—places where we can keep ourselves "salty," where we can continue to feel the typical taste of Christian life. If we don't first keep that taste in ourselves, we won't be able to offer it to the world.

Today the great solitude of people is generating new attempts at communities of belonging. Nonetheless, they usually start from important but partial aspects of life: an interest, a hobby, a particular social commitment, a value in which a person strongly believes. In this way, we create forms of coming together in which solitude is fought by being with other people, but without sharing the real drama of life, the big questions about the meaning of our existence. These are the questions that affect the religious sphere of the human being. I think we Christians have the necessary task of practicing for ourselves a different way of being together, and we have to show it to the world. We must live as brothers and sisters not because we are very close friends or share the same interests, but because we all want to build the Kingdom of God and live a holy life to reach Paradise. I believe that this strong common purpose can allow people and families to live together. Just like in monasteries, this will be possible if prayer, and nothing else, is the foundation of all life.

INTRODUCTION
By
Cameron M. Thompson

It is important to note right from the beginning that the Benedict Option, both in Benedict's own day and in our own—that is, during the collapse of the then-dominant-superpower of Rome, and in the midst of the collapse of the dominant global superpowers of today—is not fundamentally about preserving Western Civilization (as some have wrongly asserted), but rather about preserving—and indeed revivifying—the faith and culture that gave birth to it, lest our religion of Christ, as incarnated in the cultures of Western Civilization, should entirely perish along with them in their current demise.

Saint Benedict himself didn't set out to preserve the collapsing Roman empire (though his monastic movement preserved and spread Christianity across Europe, giving birth to a renascence of Christian culture), nor should we set out on the way of the Benedict Option to preserve modern Western Civilization. Indeed, the modern global West has already drifted so far from its Christian roots as to be increasingly incompatible with living true Christian life, which by its very nature carries a necessarily ecclesial dimension—that is to say Christianity cannot be lived at all without a concrete community wherein our salvation and sanctification can be worked out through a living, breathing, Christian culture.

Nor is it enough (indeed, it would be a fatal flaw) to preserve merely the historic trappings of Western Civilization, valuable though they may be. The one thing necessary, what is demanded of our times, is to reclaim and restore—in concrete communities with all the infrastructural elements required for the task—authentic Christian culture as a lived experience. This is what, in his own day, St. Benedict in fact did—*"establish a school for the service of the Lord"*—and so it is what we must set out to do in our own day. We must not mistake the flowers for the root, nor the leaf for the vital seed, and so we should not set out to preserve the perishable and temporally-situated elements of a Western Civilization that sprang from Christ, but rather preserve and nourish the vital seeds of Christian life itself, the fire of divine love, if you will, which when planted in actual living communities will bring forth a new renaissance of Christian culture and civilization that will breathe new life into the world in the days of our great grandchildren. And we owe this to them as their ancestors and their fathers and mothers in the holy and sacred Christian faith.

ACKNOWLEDGMENTS

With filial gratitude to the holy Benedict of Nursia whose wisdom has guided me from my youth, dedicated in honor of the Madonna di Loreto, to my wife and children, and to all those pursuing this way who inspired me to undertake this work.

The Original Benedict Option Guidebook

Benedict of Nursia's own Rules
for Living Christian Community
in a Post-Christian Society

1

YOUR CALLING

Listen, my child, to the teachings of the Master, and incline the ear of your heart. Receive freely and carry out effectively your loving father's instructions, that by the labor of obedience you may return to Him who you have fallen away from through the idleness of disobedience.

To you, therefore, my words are now directed, who are renouncing your own whims to do battle under the Lord Christ the True King, by taking up the strong, bright weapons of obedience.

In the first place, whatever good thing you begin to do, beg of Him with most earnest prayer to perfect it, so that He who has counted us worthy to be His sons and daughters need never be grieved by our wrongdoing.

For we must always serve Him with the good things that He has given us, that He should never as an angry father disinherit his children, nor ever as a dreadful master provoked by our wrongdoing, hand us over to everlasting punishment as wicked servants who shrank away from following Him to glory.

Let us then arise at once, for Scripture stirs us up by saying: "It is now the hour for us to rise from sleep;" and opening our eyes to the deifying light, let us hear with attentive ears the warning that the divine voice cries daily to us, saying: "If today you hear his voice, harden not your hearts." And again: "He that has ears to hear let him hear what the Spirit says to the churches." And what does He say?—"Come, my children, listen to me, and I will teach you the fear of the Lord: Run while you have the light of life, lest the darkness of death overtake you."

Commentary: *Let us listen and be attentive to the way of our fathers before us in faith, the sure way that they have trod for millennia on the path to salvation and the light of the world. Benedict is calling us here to listen with the ears of our heart to what we know in our heart to be true even if we cannot reason why or calculate out how we shall do it.*

You will see in what follows throughout the book that he doesn't leave us to figure it out for ourselves—indeed we cannot do that, as it would mean too much reliance on ourselves and our own egos. Rather he will show us the clear way to turn back to God and the simple instructions for how to restore Christian culture, first in ourselves and in our concrete communities of fellow Christians, and in this way laying the foundations for a new and brighter civilization just as the Benedictine way has always done.

We are here with Benedict under the banner of Christ because we must, to do this well, renounce our own whims, our own preferences and willfulness, and do battle using the noble weapons of obedience to One higher than ourselves, higher than any cause we may individually have.

*The **greatest** danger we face in this endeavor is not from external persecution, nor even soft totalitarianism from outside, but rather from our own fear of greatness—fear, the mind-killer, that internal saboteur who is our own smallness of heart and reluctance to follow our king to Glory.*

You have felt the call, you have come to recognize, to some degree, the urgency of our situation. That is why you are here reading this. The biggest risk you face is to let it stop there and fall back into a false sense of security, to shrink away and live as though dead to God in hardness of heart.

Benedict reminds us that we must strike while the iron of our hearts is hot, and run forward while we have yet the light of life within us. So strive forward for what lies ahead: keep your eyes on the goal and do not succumb to the darkness of soul that would lull you back into the torpor of complacency with the world and its ways.

2

THE WAY OF LIFE

And the Lord, seeking his laborer in the multitude to whom he cries out, says again: "Who is the person that would have life and desires to see good days?" If hearing this you reply, "I am," God says to you: "If you would have true and everlasting life, let your tongue speak no evil and your lips speak no deceit; turn away from evil and do good; seek after peace and pursue it. And when you have done all this, my eyes shall be upon you, and my ears open to your prayers, and before ever you call upon me I will say to you: 'Behold, here I am'."

What can be sweeter to us than this voice of the Lord inviting us? See, in His loving kindness the Lord shows us the way of life.

Therefore, having our loins girt with faith and the performance of good works, let us walk in His ways under the guidance of the Gospel, that we may be found worthy of seeing Him who has called us to His kingdom.

For if we desire to dwell in the tent of His kingdom, we must run to it through acts of good or we shall never reach it. But let us with the prophet ask the Lord, saying:

"Lord, who shall dwell in your tent, or who shall rest on your holy mountain?"

After this question, let us listen to the Lord answering and showing us the way to his tent, saying: "The one who walks without stain and practices justice, who speaks truth from his heart; who has not used his tongue for deceit, who has done no evil to his neighbor, who has not slandered his neighbor." This is the one who, in any temptation from the malicious devil, has brought it to nothing by casting the devil and his temptation out of the sight of his heart, and has laid hold of his thoughts while they were still small and has dashed them against Christ; These are the ones, who fearing the Lord, are not puffed up by their good works, but holding that the good which is in them cannot be done alone, but rather done by the Lord, they magnify the Lord working in them, saying with the prophet: "Not to us, Lord, not to us; but to your name give the glory."

Hence the Lord says in the Gospel: "Whoever hears these my words and does them, shall be like a wise man who built his house upon rock; and when the floods came, the winds blew, and they beat upon that house, it did not fall, for it was founded on a rock."

Having asked the Lord who shall dwell in his tent, and having heard his commands for any who would dwell there, if we fulfill these duties, we shall be heirs of the kingdom of heaven. Therefore, our hearts and our bodies must be prepared to do battle under holy obedience to his commands; and for that which our nature finds barely possible to do, let us ask the Lord that he will help us with his grace to accomplish.

Commentary: *Here Benedict identifies for us just what is the way of life entailed by the Benedict Option: what are we even called to do? how are we to live? and practically speaking, how are we to go about doing it?*

It's beautiful: Benedict teaches us first the principle and foundation for our work—without which nothing else is possible and all else is doomed to fail. That is, we must—each and every one of us who would take up the Benedict Option, and cooperatively together within our respective communities—first and foremost seek God.

The call starts with a very simple reminder of why we are exploring (even living) the Benedict Option: the simple reason that we "would have life and desire to see good days." And so Benedict answers us with the words of God Himself telling us the very simple thing we must do if we would seek after true and everlasting life: "let your tongue speak no evil and your lips speak no deceit; turn away from evil and do good; seek after peace and pursue it."

*The requirements for admission to dwelling in the tent of the Lord are indeed a tall order for us, that in every aspect of our endeavor we must never depart from God's requirement that we "walk without stain and practice justice, speak the truth from our heart (in other words, live not by lies), use not our tongue for deceit, do no evil to our neighbor, nor slander our neighbor." And we must maintain a continual awareness in the depths of our being that the Benedict Option **isn't our own work, but God's work of good for us and through us**.*

The moral and religious duties Benedict identifies here are really quite simple, and if we carry them out truly, we will already be dwelling in the Kingdom of God. But to truly do so requires us to battle with the demons and temptations of our own fallen nature and so we must be prepared to do battle under obedience to the Lord; St. Benedict the holy teacher shows us here the sure way that has guided our Christian forebears for the last 1,500 years.

3

TO LEAD IS TO SERVE

The abbot who is worthy to be over a monastery should always be mindful of what he is called, and fulfill in his actions the meaning of the title he bears as 'superior' (that is, he or she must be held to a higher standard).

Therefore, the abbot should never teach, establish, or urge anything contrary to the Lord's precepts; but his commands and teaching should be a leaven of divine justice into the minds of his disciples.

Likewise the abbot should always bear in mind that in the tremendous judgment of God he will be examined on two things: both his own teaching and the obedience of his disciples, and he should know that whatever flaw the master of the house finds in the sheep will be laid to blame on the shepherd.

On the other hand he will be blameless, if he cared for a restless and disobedient flock with all pastoral diligence and tried every remedy for their corrupt activities; so that he may be acquitted at the Lord's judgment seat and say to the Lord with the Prophet: "I have not hid your justice within my heart. I have declared your truth and your salvation... But they have disdainfully disregarded me."

Therefore, anyone who receives the title of abbot should govern his disciples with a twofold teaching: that is, show them what is good and holy by his deeds even more than by his words. So that he may teach the intelligent disciples the commandments of God through his words and the simpler disciples through his actions.

He should show his disciples by his example that what he has taught them to be contrary to God's law is not to be done, lest despite preaching to others, he himself should be proved faithless.

He should make no distinction of persons in the monastery. He should not love one more than another, unless it be because they are better in good works and obedience. Let him not prefer one of noble blood over one who is a former slave without some other good cause.

But if for a just reason the abbot considers it appropriate to make such a distinction, he may do so in regard to the rank of anyone. Otherwise let everyone keep his own place; for "whether slave or free, we are all one in Christ," and we all bear an equal burden of service under one Lord, "for there is no distinction of rank in the sight of God."

Only in this way are we distinguished before God, if we are found to excel others in good works and in humility. Therefore, let the abbot have equal love for all, and impose the same discipline for all according to their merit.

In his teaching the abbot should always follow the example of the Apostle where he says: "Reprove, entreat, rebuke," that is, mixing at one time and another gentleness and severity, as the occasion requires. He should show the severity of a master and the loving affection of a father. That is to say, he must sternly rebuke the undisciplined and the restless; but the obedient, meek, and patient he must gently encourage to become better. But we exhort him to rebuke swiftly the negligent and disdainful.

The more honest and those of good understanding, he should correct the first and second time only with words; but he should curb the arrogant and cruel at the very first offense with more severe punishment.

The abbot should always keep in mind what he is and what he is called, and to know that to whom much has been entrusted, from him much will be required; and he should know what a difficult and arduous thing it is to take on, leading others and adapting his approach for a variety of characters and temperaments.

He must adjust and adapt himself to serve the needs of all —to one gentle words, to another stern correction, and to still another with persuasive discussion, to each one according to their temperament and intelligence—so that there not only be no loss, but even rejoice in the increase of gain.

Above all things, the abbot must not neglect or undervalue the wellbeing of those entrusted to him. As a leader he must not have too great a concern about fleeting, earthly, perishable things; but he should always keep in mind that he has undertaken the leadership of other human beings, for whose wellbeing he will be held accountable.

He should not complain for lack of material means, and he should remember what is written: "Seek first the kingdom of God and his righteousness, and all these things shall be added unto you." And again: "There is no lack to those who fear the Lord."

He who becomes a leader of others must prepare himself to give an account for them; and whatever the number of those he has in his care, it is certain that on judgment day he will, without doubt, have to give an account to the Lord for all these men and women, in addition to an account of his own soul.

Commentary: *Every community necessarily has people in positions of leadership. Any Benedict Option community will need to have true leaders. In this chapter St. Benedict shows us what a true leader is, and what is required of the faithful, walking according to the path that he has shown us.*

It is a serious and weighty thing to undertake the governance and leadership of other men and women. And yet, if such a task falls to you, or God's providence places you in such an office, then you must undertake diligently the task appointed you for the salvation and divinization of those entrusted to your care.

A leader must guide and direct his or her people as an act of service—the service of drawing out the greatness in each one of them, of cultivating their talents and helping them carry out the life mission that God has given them. Such a leader's task is "to govern all things well so that the weak have nothing to run away from and the strong have something to strive for."

A Christian leader's primary responsibility is to provide what is necessary, insofar as it is in his or her power, for their people to achieve their salvation and become truly free to serve God with all their heart, soul, and mind. Any leader following the way of the holy Benedict must know also that they must govern their people with the twofold teaching of both their word and their action, that is, a leader in a Benedict Option community must live single-mindedly in Christ, loving God with their whole being, and their neighbor as another self. Know that any leader within such a community must be held to a higher standard of Christian discipleship, and must keep constantly before his or her eyes his or her own moral frailty and need for God's grace and for unceasing prayer.

And so anyone in leadership within a community of the Christian faithful must truly love those they serve in their leadership; which means that they need to truly know them, and so be able to serve them well according to the needs and temperament of each. A leader must be at one and the same time both a severe task-master and a loving father or mother. As a leader, you—yes, you, for the very reading of this places upon your shoulders the responsibility of some level of leadership—must devote extra care to leaning in to the love of God through interior prayer of the heart, and learn to love your people with the heart of Christ.

Above all, Benedict reminds us, the people you serve as a leader—those for whom you bear responsibility—are human beings made in the image and likeness of God, and their needs are for more than merely earthly gain: you are responsible for their whole wellbeing. Each one entrusted to you has an eternal destiny to fulfill, known fully only to God alone, and you will be called by God to account for them—each and every one—in addition to accounting for your own life. Indeed, at all times and in all places you already stand before the judgment seat of Christ.

And so you must engrave in your heart that no matter the temptations, distractions, and assaults of the evil one, you and the whole community you lead must "seek first and foremost the kingdom of God and his righteousness, and all these things (i.e. earthly needs) will be added unto you."

4

VALUING COUNSEL

Whenever something important needs to be done, let the abbot call together the whole community, and discuss the issue that is at hand.

Having heard their views, he should weigh the matter in his own mind and do what seems best. However, we said all should be called for advice because the Lord often reveals to the younger what is best.

They should, however, give their advice with humility, and not presume to stubbornly defend their own point of view, for the final say must depend on the abbot's decision, so that they obey what he ultimately decides is best for all.

But just as it is fitting that disciples obey their master, so it is fitting that the master provide for all things with prudence and justice. Therefore, let all follow this Rule as their guide in everything, and let no one rashly depart from it.

Therefore, the abbot should do everything with a healthy reverence for the Lord and in observance of the Rule, knowing that, beyond a doubt, he will have to give an account to God, the most just Judge, for all his decisions.

If, however, there are smaller and less important matters to be decided on, he only needs to take counsel with the senior members, keeping in mind it is written: "Do all things with counsel, and you will not regret what you have done."

Commentary: *Now that Benedict has shown us the qualities required of leaders within the Christian community—the character and considerations necessary for leadership in the Benedictine way—he moves on to show us the application within the community of the humility required of a leader. We see here that community governance and the role of leadership is not for the individual leader alone as a sole actor, but rather that deliberation and decision-making have a profoundly communitarian—indeed, ecclesial—dimension, though each community member has their own particular role in the process.*

Notice that for important decisions and courses of action that need to be taken, a Benedict Option leader should call together the entire community—even the young—to discuss the matter over and consider all aspects of the issue at hand. Benedict specifically mentions the Biblical precedent that God often reveals to the young what is the best course of action. And this is not without reason: youth are more naturally inclined to greatness of spirit where older persons often have grown "too practical" and faint-hearted to naturally incline towards the magnanimity God demands of us.

Benedict does not, however, advise us to to be democratic as such, for this is not of itself necessarily the Christian way. Rather, it should look like this: all members of the community having had their say and given their input and advice, the elected leader—who holds the place of the authority of Christ the Servant in the community—must weigh the matter and come to a wise decision that he or she, having taken into account all that the community members have said, and like a loving and prudent mother or father having considered the needs of each person, believes to be the right course of action for the salvation and sanctification of each of the members of the community.

And lest pride, personal whims, base desires, vanity, or some other weakness should tempt you as a Benedict Option leader or cloud your judgment, you must keep in mind that you will have to answer to God for whatever you decide and for whatever course of action you take.

Note that even in smaller matters, it is important that the Benedictine leader take counsel with others (even if only the senior members of the community). This is not so as to be inefficient, or—God forbid—delay, but rather to assure that the leader makes decisions well and isn't merely relying on his or her own wisdom and limited perspective. Thus leaders within a Benedict Option community should appoint advisors and delegate other subordinate roles within the community to share in the decision-making, governance, and leadership of the community.

5

THE TOOLS FOR LIVING WELL

*After giving us the foundations of Benedict Option leadership and community governance, and before launching into the in-depth treatise on the practical pursuit of true Christian humility (the heart of the deifying transformation in Christ and the primary arena of our spiritual warfare against sin) which follows in the next chapter, Benedict lays out for us a series of simple admonitions—indeed a re-collection of the Lord's precepts—that serve as **the** tool-set of the "spiritual craft" of living well. These "tools," as Benedict himself calls them, are the primary instruments in day-to-day life for the great work of spiritual endeavor we are called to do.*

In the first place to love the Lord your God with all your heart, all your soul, and all your strength.

Then, your neighbor as yourself.

Then, to not kill, to not commit adultery, to not steal, to not desire to possess something that you do not have.

To not give false testimony, to honor all men, and to not do to another what you would not have done to yourself, and to turn away from yourself in order to follow Christ.

To keep your body in check, not seeking after pleasures.

To love fasting, to restore the poor to good condition,

to clothe the naked, to visit the sick, to bury the dead.

To help those in trouble, to console the sorrowing, to keep yourself a stranger to the ways of this passing age, and to prefer nothing to the love of Christ.

To not give way to wrath, to not hold a grudge, to not hold deceit in your heart, to not make a false peace, to not neglect charity.

To not make an oath, lest you commit perjury, but to speak the truth with both heart and tongue.

To not return evil for evil, to do no harm but even bear patiently the harm done to you.

To love your enemies, to not curse those who curse you, but rather to bless them, and to bear persecution for the sake of justice.

To not be proud, nor an alcoholic, nor an over-eater.

To not be sleepy, to not be lazy, to not be a grumbler, to not be a detractor.

To put your trust in God, to attribute to God, rather than to yourself, the good you see in yourself, but to recognize that any evil is your own doing and take responsibility for it.

To hold in fear and awe the day of judgment, to dread Gehenna, to desire eternal life with all the longing of your spirit.

To keep death daily before your eyes, to keep watch at all times over the actions of your life, to know for certain that God gazes upon you in every place.

To dash at once against Christ the evil thoughts that come into your heart, and to disclose them to your spiritual father or mother.

To keep your tongue from wicked and perverse speech, to not love a lot of speaking, to not utter empty words or those fit for laughter, nor to love excessive or boisterous laughter.

To listen eagerly to the holy readings, to lean frequently on prayer.

To confess your past sins with sighs and tears daily to God in prayer, and to correct them for the future.

To not carry out the desires of the flesh, and to be averse to your own whims.

To obey the orders of the abbot in all things, even though he himself might act otherwise, mindful of the Lord's admonition: "What they say, do ye; but what they do, do ye not."

To not desire to be called holy before you really are; but to actually be holy first, so that you can truly be called holy.

To fulfill the commandments of God in your daily activities, to love chastity, to hate no one, to not have jealousy, to not exercise envy, to not love contention, and to flee from flattery.

To honor your elders, to love your juniors, to pray for your enemies in the love of Christ, to make peace with someone whom you've quarreled with before the setting of the sun, and to never despair of the mercy of God.

Behold, these are the tools of the spiritual craft, which, if they have been applied unceasingly day and night, and are given back to the Master on judgment day, will merit for us from the Lord the reward that he promised: "Which eye has not seen, nor the ear heard, what God has prepared for those who love Him."

Commentary: *The imagery Benedict employs here illustrates the beautiful metaphor that recapitulates the wisdom of generations of the monastic masters of Christian life that came before him: that* **we are co-artisans with Christ in crafting our lives**—*ultimately the work of the Holy Spirit— and we employ these "tools" under the guidance of our masters and teachers in the Christian life within the workshop of the* **Master Craftsman**, *our heavenly Father.*

6

OBEDIENCE

The first step of humility is obedience without delay. This is fitting for those who consider nothing to be dearer to them than Christ: those who, because of the holy service which they have promised, or from the dread of hell or the longing for the glory of eternal life, receive any order from their superior as though it were a divine command, and take no delay in doing it.

Such people instantly leave their own concerns and cast aside their own whims and, dropping everything and leaving their own tasks unfinished, follow through promptly and accomplish what was asked of them. Thus, as if in the same moment, both the master's request and the disciple's finished work are, in the speed of reverence for God, swiftly brought together. Thus does the desire for eternal life move them.

However, this obedience is only acceptable to God and pleasing to others if the orders are done without hesitation, delay, lukewarmness, grumbling or complaint, because obedience offered to legitimate authority is obedience shown to God, for he himself has said: "Whoever hears you hears me."

Moreover, obedience is a blessing to be shown by all not only to the abbot, but also to one another as brothers, since we know that it is by this way of mutual obedience that we advance toward God.

Therefore, although orders of the abbot or his appointed provosts take precedence over any unofficial order, in every instance the junior members should obey the senior members with love and devotion.

Commentary: *The very heart and soul of the Benedict Option (and of any Christian community that follows that strategy) is the interior sanctification of each member of the community. The whole purpose of the Benedict Option is, after all, (both in St. Benedict's own day and our own) to create spaces where Christians can be truly free to worship God and in community live a life conducive to their sanctification and indeed their deification.*

*The holy Benedict begins here a series of chapters that lead us up the staircase of Divine Ascent: **Obedience**, **Silence**, **Humility**, and **Prayer**. Obedience is for St. Benedict—and thus for anyone opting to follow his path—not only a private matter nor even a merely vertical matter, but rather a multi-directional thing. In other words, obedience is to be given not only to God, not only to his authoritative representative the abbot (or whatever title a leader in a BenOp community might hold), but also between the community members themselves as among equals. It is thus not only a matter of personal sanctification, but also a vital dimension of community life (which is likewise true for silence, humility, and prayer).*

Benedict points out that prompt obedience to the will of God is the most natural thing for someone to whom nothing is dearer than Christ—even to prefer nothing to the love of Christ (as was said in the preceding chapter)—those who care to do the will of God the Father rather than caring so much to do their own will. But the question is: how are we to know the will of God in everyday life? Well, that is a matter of discernment to be sure, but a clear indicator given to us by the wisdom of the holy monastic fathers throughout the ages is that

God rewards obedience (to legitimate authorities) for its own sake. Many saints have called authentic obedience "the clearest path to sanctity" but also "the rarest virtue of our day." It is a concept utterly foreign to the anti-hierarchical paradigm of liberalism and individualism, but as Benedict shows us here, Christian obedience is in fact the furthest thing from oppression, and rather than stifling us, actually gives us great freedom in the face of oppression.

This is because obedience, rightly understood, isn't the oppression of our will, but rather its genuine liberation. You see, we are all of us already (whether we realize it or not) obedient to either the world or Christ, either to our own whims or to the will of God our loving Father. Obedience to Christ does not chain us to something lower than ourselves, but rather is an obedience to a higher command—a higher authority than the demands of the powers of this world, and so actually frees us from slavery to any lesser thing beneath God. Obedience to God (and his mediated authority in the hierarchy of His created order) in fact gives us the strength necessary to break the bonds that chain us to what is beneath us.

*To be perfectly obedient and to be totally reliant on God— true abandonment to divine providence—are one and the same thing. This prompt obedience to the will of God that Benedict describes here means to become like the angels of heaven, who obey and carry out in the self-same moment the very command. In this way we would fulfill the very thing we pray for when we say "Thy will be done **on earth as it is in heaven.**"*

Finally, we see here the fundamental principle of organizing a Christian community—indeed a whole Christian civilization: nobody is above obedience; even the head of the whole Christian people (and of course any leader of a Benedict Option community) must be obedient to the rule that Benedict in his wisdom lays out here, and ultimately obedient to God. Indeed, the act of Christian leadership itself demands profound obedience even to the duty of serving the needs of the community.

Even the most removed and remote single person should be be obedient to God's providence and to the demands of his or her own vocation and mission if they would live a Christian life and become holy. How much more so is it the case for those who live in Christian society with others, as is the goal of the Benedict Option? What greater principle for community cohesion and charitable relationships could one choose than the mutual obedience urged by the holy Benedict? What greater principle of unity? Such mutual obedience among brothers and sisters in Christ, together under obedience to Christ our true king (see chapter 1) is a more authentic liberty, a greater safeguard of authentic equality before God and man, and a more genuine brotherhood in the Body of Christ, than the false gods that revolutionary secularism offers with its counterfeit epithet to these values.[5] On the contrary, behold how sweet and pleasant it is when brothers dwell in such unity[6] as that proposed by the way of the holy Benedict!

---

[5] cf. the motto of the revolutionaries of *"liberty, equality, and fraternity"*

[6] cf. Psalm 133

7

THE SPIRIT OF SILENCE

We should imitate the prophet who declared: "I have said, I will guard my ways, so that I do no wrong with my tongue: I have set a guard over my mouth. I was silent and am humbled, and keep quiet even about good things." Here the prophet shows that, if at times we need to refrain from speaking even of good things for the sake of silence, all the more should we abstain from evil words on account of the punishment due to sin.

It is written: "In talking a lot you will not escape sin," and elsewhere: "Death and life lie in the power of the tongue."

For it is the role to the teacher to speak and to educate; it is therefore right for the disciple to be silent and to hear.

Commentary: *In order to be sufficiently free from distractions and egotism to become capable of true and prompt obedience to the will of God, it is a necessary prerequisite that we cultivate silence and stillness, both exterior and interior. We must cultivate stillness and silence so as to hear the word of God that we might do it.*

Especially in the hyper-textual noisiness of modern society, it is of the utmost importance that we should, as Christian communities, if we would truly follow the way of Benedict as a strategy in a post-Christian world, extricate ourselves not only from those activities and institutions that explicitly render us incapable of Christian living, but also extricate ourselves from the all-pervasive noise and bustle of contemporary anti-culture that penetrates all aspects of modern conventional living. If we are to recover and live authentic Christian culture—to say nothing even of a life of prayer—we must rediscover what it means to be human by entering into the spirit of silence and calm.

The Sacred Scriptures, and the consistent teaching of the church fathers and mothers seem to indicate that all too often too much is said and not enough is done in practice. We need to return to the **practice** *of Christian life, and not merely talk about it—and this return to the practice of Christian life can only be accomplished by forming concrete localized communities. Moreover, God tells us that "death and life lie in the power of the tongue."[7] Sin is unavoidable in too much talking (and writing, and texting), and so even pleasant conversation should give way to peaceful silence. As the holy monastic father Ephrem the Syrian said, "edifying spiritual conversation is like precious silver, but silence is like pure gold."*

If we would truly learn the way of eternal life, truly hear the word of God and how He wills to incarnate a new birth of Christian civilization through us, we must be like good disciples: we must be silent and listen to the words of Christ the Master.

---

[7] Proverbs 18:21

8

THE LADDER OF HUMILITY

"Whoever exalts himself shall be humbled; and whoever humbles himself shall be exalted."

"I have sought with humility rather than exalting myself, and you have rewarded my soul like a weaning infant on his mother's breast."

If we wish to reach the summit of humility, and arrive swiftly at that heavenly height which is climbed in the present life only by humility, then, ascending by our actions, we must set up the ladder which appeared to Jacob in his dream, by means of which angels were shown to him ascending and descending. Without a doubt, it is understood that this ascending and descending means that we descend by pride and ascend by humility.

The ladder set up for us, however, is our life in the world, whereon the humble heart is lifted up by the Lord into heaven. The two poles of this ladder are our body and our soul; and into the midst of these poles our divine calling has inserted different degrees of humility, which are rungs that must be climbed.

The first degree of humility, then, is that a person always keep the fear of God before his eyes, and flee from any forgetfulness of it. He should always be mindful of all that God has instructed. Now, in order to always be on guard against evil thoughts, he should always say in his heart: "If I will keep myself from iniquity, then I will be spotless before him."

The second degree of humility is that a person not love his own will nor delight in satisfying his own desires, but models his actions on the Lord's saying: "I did not come to do my own will, but the will of him who sent me." It is likewise written: "Willfulness brings a penalty, but doing what is necessary wins the crown."

The third degree of humility is that for the love of God a person place himself in all obedience under an elder, imitating the Lord, of whom the Apostle says: "He became obedient even unto death."

The fourth degree of humility is that if, in this obedience, a person faces difficult and unpleasant things, or even any injury, he embrace them with patience and stillness of mind, and hold out to the end, rather than grow weary and give up, for Scripture says: "Whoever perseveres to the end will be saved," and again: "Let your heart be strengthened, and wait for the Lord."

The fifth degree of humility is that a person hide none of the evil thoughts that come into his heart nor any wrongdoing committed by him in secret, but rather to humbly confess them to his abbot. Scripture exhorts us about this, saying: "Reveal your way to the Lord and trust in him," and further, "Confess to the Lord, for he is good, for his mercy endures forever." Likewise the prophet says: "I have acknowledged my faults to you and I have not covered up my wrongdoing."

The sixth degree of humility is that a monk be content in all things with the poorest and worst conditions, and in everything imposed on him to consider himself like a poor and undeserving workman, saying with the prophet: "I am reduced to nothing and was ignorant; I am like a beast of burden next to you, and I am always with you."

The seventh degree of humility is that a person considers himself to be lower ranking and more dispensable than all others, not merely saying this with his tongue, but even passionately believing it in the depths of his heart, humbling himself and saying with the prophet: "I am a worm and no man, one scorned by mankind and the outcast of the commoners." "After having risen high, I have been humbled and brought to confusion," and also: "It is good for me that you have humbled me, so that I may learn your commandments."

The eighth degree of humility is when a monk does only what is recommended by the common rule of the monastery and the example of those greater than he.

The ninth degree of humility is that a monk keep his tongue from speaking, and in keeping silence speaks when asked; for scripture shows that "in talking a lot there is no escape from sin," and that "a talkative man is not stable on the earth."

The tenth degree of humility is for a person to not be easy and quick to laughter, for it is written: "The fool raises his voice when he laughs (but a wise man smiles quietly)."

The eleventh degree of humility is that when a monk speaks, he do so gently and without joking, humbly and with gravity or few words and reasonable speech. Also he should not speak in a loud voice, as it is written: "The wise man is recognized by the fewness of his words."

The twelfth degree of humility is when a monk is humble not only in his heart, but always shows humility in his posture and deportment. Wherever he may be, sitting, walking, or standing, he should always have his head bowed down, his gaze fixed on the ground, considering himself to be already present before the judgment seat of God, and always saying to himself in his heart what the publican in the Gospel said, with his eyes fixed on the ground: "Lord, I am not worthy, as a sinner, to lift up my eyes to the heavens." and again with the prophet: "I am bowed down and humbled everywhere."

Therefore, having ascended all these rungs of the ladder of humility, the person will immediately arrive at that perfect love of God that casts out fear. Because of this love, all things which at first he did only out of fear, he will now begin to do easily as second nature and through habit. He will do this now no longer from the fear of Gehenna, but out of love for Christ, from the very habit and experience of the good and delight in virtue.

Commentary: *Here at the very heart of his guide to Christian life in community (which is thus also a guide for Christian society in general), St. Benedict places **the very heart of true Christian life**: the Way of Virtue and the Way of Prayer—this chapter and the next. The Way of Virtue—the natural characteristics of human excellence that can be acquire by habit—is contained entirely within this exposition on the development of humility, the fundamental virtue of the heart and "gateway" of all the other virtues. In the next chapter we will see the Way of Prayer and the secret to prayer for both the personal and the community/societal dimensions of life (which, though distinct, are inseparable).*

Benedict uses the imagery of the mystical ladder that Jacob saw in his dream of angels descending and ascending, which Christ also referred to himself in his calling of the apostle Nathanael. Benedict identifies that this ladder is the true key to understanding our life in this world, and that our body and soul are the two railings in the staircase or poles of the ladder by which we either climb or descend (by either humility or pride). A complex metaphor to understand in application, to be sure, but thankfully we are not left without practical instructions, for like a kindly and loving master, Benedict proceeds to describe for us in concrete ways the practical "rungs" of the ladder which must be climbed in order to reach perfection and transformation in Christ.

He does this, however, in a way that may not be immediately obvious to our modern minds. He has actually inverted the order of the steps by which we might develop humility, beginning rather with the pinnacle or highest "rung" as the first degree in the order presented above. He nonetheless tells us (in an encoded way) at the start of the chapter that he was going to do this—which you can see if you follow his alternating inversions of the terms 'ascending' and 'descending'. In Appendix 2 you will find the list that shows the sequence of these steps according to how we actually develop humility—the Way of Virtue—in a practical way, that is the reverse of the order listed above.

Benedict concludes with a spiritual reflection on the ladder: that once we have arrived at the top of the ladder—which, truly speaking, is a continual process of ascent and descent (and ascent by descent) that we will carry out for our whole life, ascending ever higher into God—then we will have trained our hearts to desire Christ alone with that perfect love of God which drives out fear. Why is this? Because true fear of the Lord (the top rung of the ladder of humility) means to fear nothing that is not God. This means that in true fear of the Lord, we have within us One who is greater than the world. This is an immense power to help us overcome sin and stand in faithfulness to God in the face of threats from the enemies of God in this world.

And thus it is this true and perfect love of God (a gift of the Holy Spirit) that unites us to God himself in Christ—because love is fundamentally a unitive force—that is the source and wellspring of all other virtues. You will note, too, how each of these steps of the ladder, though expressed in the level of the individual person, necessarily entail a community or social dimension. **This cannot be done alone, but only in community with others.**

9

ON PRAYER

On account of the thorns of scandal that are bound to spring up, the morning and the evening prayers should never pass without the Lord's Prayer being said by the leader in its place at the end so that all can hear it. This is so that those gathered may renew the covenant they make and when they say, "forgive us as we forgive" they may cleanse themselves of failings in this regard.

As the prophet says, "seven times a day I have praised you," this sacred sevenfold number will be fulfilled by us if we perform the office of our prayers at the times of morning, the first hour, third hour, midday, ninth hour, evening, and at day's-end. It was of these times of day that it is said, "seven times a day I have praised you." Now, the same prophet says of the night watches: "At midnight I got up to proclaim you." At these times, therefore, we should offer praise to our Creator "for the judgments of his justice."[8]

---

[8] In Appendix 3 you will find a chart that shows the times of day to which these hours of prayer correspond.

We believe that the divine presence is everywhere and that "the eyes of the Lord behold the good and the bad in every place." We should especially believe this without any doubt when we are assisting in the divine office. We must always be mindful of what the prophet says: "Serve the Lord with reverence," and "sing psalms attentively." And, "I will sing praise to you in the sight of the angels." Therefore, we should consider how we should behave in the sight of God and his angels, and we should stand to sing our psalms in such a way that our mind is in harmony with our voice.

If we do not presume to approach people in positions of power for a favor, except with humility and reverence, how much the more so should we approach the Lord God of all things to ask things of him with humility and purity of devotion?

Know that it is not in much speaking, but in the purity of heart and tears of compunction that our prayers are heard. For this reason prayer should be short and pure, unless it happens to be prolonged by a strong inspiration of divine grace moving the heart.

Let the time and space for prayer be dedicated to what it is for, and let nothing else be done or stored there. When the Work of God (i.e. the liturgy of the hours) is finished, all should exit in deep silence, and showing reverence to God; that a member who perhaps desires particularly to pray in private is not distracted by another's misconduct. But if someone desires to pray alone in private, he should enter the space with simplicity and pray, not with a loud voice, but with tears and fervor of heart.

As soon as a person hears the call to pray the divine office, he should immediately set aside whatever task is at hand and swiftly make haste to the place of prayer, yet with gravity and without silliness. Indeed, nothing is to be preferred to (i.e. "put ahead of") the Work of God.

Commentary: *Though in the original formatting and layout of Benedict's Rule he devotes multiple chapters to which psalms should be prayed at what hours, and includes remarks about the nature of prayer throughout many other chapters on other subjects besides, I have collected all of the principal texts on prayer here in one place (aside from the formal prescription on which psalms to pray at what time, which even Benedict himself says should be ordered differently according to the needs of the particular community). I have nonetheless retained in this present edition Benedict's original structure of the work as a whole in having this chapter on prayer right in the middle of the book, paired with the chapter on humility, just as Benedict has in his original. Why are these two chapters coupled together? Because while the ladder of humility— the Way of Virtue—deals with training our human nature, the Way of Prayer deals with the order of grace, and how to structure our time and space both personally and as a community, to respond to that grace.*

What wisdom—not only theological, but in terms of community leadership, peace and social cohesion—Benedict shares with us in emphasizing the clear primacy of place of the Our Father, and specifically the place of the sacred petition "forgive us inasmuch as we forgive others." This prayer thus reminds the members of the community daily—twice a day, in fact—of the need to forgive one another from the heart, and cultivate the right relationships of true peace with one another who are children of the same Heavenly Father.

When Benedict identifies the seven times throughout the day (and once in the night) that we should offer the formal prayers of the liturgical office, it is important to note that in practice the specific times for these prayers varied according to the season—that is, according to the times of sunrise and sunset. This seasonal variation conforms the rhythms of Christian life at its very heart—prayer—to the cyclical rhythms of God's creation, which is an aspect of traditional Christian living and worship that we would do very well to recover within our communities.

Having such times of prayer organized at a central chapel for the community removes the great burden of each family having to organize the time and space for these prayers on their own for themselves. A note of practical advice for a community would be to arrange set times and a central location for common prayer to take place during the traditional hours of the day—at minimum the morning prayers and evening prayers—and so provide the families of the community **at least the opportunity** for this liturgy of the hours without obliging everyone to be present, respecting the freedom of the families and individuals to attend to their various needs and schedules on any given day, participating when they are able.

After identifying the times when the community should gather for prayer, Benedict shows us that the divine presence is everywhere, and thus that the present-state awareness of this fact throughout our everyday life is also a fundamental part of attaining interior prayer of the heart and true sanctity. Naturally, it is of course much easier to have this continual awareness if we are surrounded in our physical and social environment by formative reminders of God's presence throughout our day.

Benedict originally planned for those seeking the Christian way of life to be praying the entire psalter each week in the course of these daily liturgical prayers of the hours, and he cites the fact that the ancient fathers of the church used to recite the entire psalter each day. What can we learn from this? Why are the psalms so important in the life of the Christian community—what is the spirituality of the psalter? The ancient sense of the church has always been that the singing of the psalms has a privileged place in Christian life, as they are in fact the prayer of the Holy Spirit himself, as the living word of God, inspired by God, and breathed ('breath' in biblical languages being the same word as 'spirit') through us into creation when we pray them. This singing of the psalms in a liturgical setting is seen to be one with the heavenly liturgy of the resurrected body of Christ, and in a very practical way is the formative Word of God that, dwelling within us by daily recitation, shapes our hearts, our communities, and our culture.

10

DELEGATION:
SHARING RESPONSIBILITY

If the community is large, those of good reputation and a holy way of life should be chosen from among them to be appointed deans, that is, leaders for teams of ten; and let them care for their teams in everything according to the commandments of God and the directions of the abbot.

Let those chosen as deans be persons the abbot may confide in sharing his burden of leadership. They should not be chosen for their rank, but for the merit of their life and the wisdom of their teaching.

If any of them should become inflated with pride and, after having been corrected even unto a third time, refuses to amend, he should be removed from office, and one who is more worthy be appointed to replace him.

Additionally, the abbot should appoint those whose life and character are secure and reliable to be responsible for the monastery resources such as tools, clothing, and things generally, and he should assign to them, as he sees fit, responsibility for all the items which must be collected after use and stored away.

Someone should be chosen from the community as cellarer of the monastery who is wise, of mature character, sober, not a great eater, nor conceited, irritable, resentful, sluggish, or wasteful, but one who has a healthy fear of God, who can be like a father to the whole community.

This cellarer should bear responsibility for everything. He should do nothing without the direction of the abbot, he should care well for what has been entrusted to him and not grieve his brothers. If a brother should perhaps request anything of him unreasonably he should not disappoint the brother by a cold refusal, but decline the inappropriate request reasonably and with humility.

He should take care to provide for the sick, the children, the guests, and the poor, with all solicitude, knowing without doubt, that he will have to give an account of all these things on judgment day. He should view all the vessels of the monastery along with their contents as though they were the sacred vessels of the altar.

Let him neglect nothing. He should become neither greedy nor wasteful, nor a squanderer of the monastery's resources; but rather he should diligently see to all things in due measure and according to the direction of the abbot.

Above all, he must have humility; and if he has nothing else to give, let him answer with a benediction, for it is written: "A benediction is above the best gift." Let him have responsibility for everything that the abbot has entrusted to him, and not presume to meddle with matters forbidden him.

He should give the brethren their appointed portion without a ruffle or delay, so that they may not be made to stumble, mindful of the divine words about the punishment of "he who causes one of these little ones to stumble: it would be better for him that a millstone be tied around his neck and he be thrown into the depths of the sea."

If the community is large, let assistants be given to him too, that by means of their help, he may fulfill the office entrusted to him with equanimity. Let the things that are to be given be distributed at the proper times, and the things that are to be requested asked for at the proper times, so that nobody may be disturbed or grieved in the house of God.

Let the brethren serve each other so that no one be excused from the service in the kitchen, except on account of sickness or for some more necessary work, because greater merit and more charity is gained through this service. Help should be given to the weak, however, that they may not do this work in sadness. Indeed, let all have help according to the size of the community and the circumstances of the place.

Let those who are to go out of the weekly service rotation do the cleaning on Saturday. He should launder the towels with which the brethren wash their hands and feet. Let both the one rotating out, as well as the one rotating in, wash the feet of all. He should return the utensils of his service to the cellarer clean and intact. Let the cellarer then be the one to give these to the server coming in, so that he may know what he gives out and what he receives back.

It all to often happens that grave scandals arise in monasteries out of the appointment of the provost. This is because there are some who, inflated with the wicked spirit of pride and thinking of themselves as second abbots, set up a despotic rule, foster scandals, and provoke dissension in the community, and especially in those places where the provost is appointed by the same person(s) who appointed the abbot.

It can easily be seen how absurd this practice is, because from the very beginning of the provost's appointment, it gives him plenty of occasion to become arrogant, when his thoughts suggest to him that he is now exempt from the authority of the abbot, because "you have been appointed too by the same person(s) who appointed the abbot." This gives rise in his heart to envy, detraction, rivalry, dissension, and general disorder.

We see, therefore, that for the preservation of peace and charity it is best that the whole government of the monastery should be in the hands of the abbot; and if it can be done, the affairs of the monastery (as we have explained before) should be attended to by deans, as the abbot shall set up. In this way, the responsibility being shared by many should keep any one individual from becoming proud.

If, however, the place should require it, or the community reasonably and with humility request it, and the abbot considers it advisable, then the abbot himself should appoint as provost someone of his own choosing, with the advice of God-fearing brothers. But let the provost reverently do whatever has been entrusted to him by the abbot, doing nothing against the abbot's will or direction, for the higher he is placed above others, the more carefully should he observe the precepts of the Rule.

Let a wise elderly person be placed at the door of the monastery as porter, one who knows how to take a message and give a reply, and whose mature age does not permit him to just wander about.

This porter should have a room near the door—or house by the gate—so that those who come may always find someone present from whom they may get an answer. As soon as anyone knocks or a poor person calls, let the porter answer with, "Thanks be to God," or ask a blessing, and with the meekness of the fear of God let him return an answer speedily and with warm affection. If the porter is in need of help, let him have a younger member of the community assigned to assist him.

Commentary: *Here Benedict teaches us not only of the practical necessity of delegation and its intrinsic excellence as flowing from humility on the part of community leadership, but also identifies a number of vital key roles that need to be fulfilled for the healthy, practical day-to-day functioning of a community. It should go without saying that Benedict holds that both women and men are equally capable of fulfilling all of these roles, including community leadership and governance in positions equivalent to abbot or provost. He articulates the necessity for delegated leadership roles as a community grows: to ensure subsidiarity on a human scale; the respective roles of those appointed over various divisions of tasks such as tools, clothing, and food; the qualities required of persons in these roles; and the need for even these helpers to have helpers. And throughout all this practical organization of roles, Benedict roots it all in the example of Christ, and out of concern for the fundamental peace and stability so necessary for community life and social cohesion—that very natural pre-requisite for authentic communion in Christ.*

There is a particular emphasis on kitchen service as a great service, because they prepare food to nourish the community in body and soul. Although particulars may differ in a community outside of a monastery, the principles seen at work here will still apply, albeit in ways appropriate to the particular arrangements and needs of the community. It would be good if all members of the community should be involved in some way at various points throughout the year in food production, preparation, and attending to the setup and cleanup and service of special meals and feasts. Not everybody need be a cook, but it is good for a community if everyone has some connection or other to the basic human practice of culinary culture.

It is worth noting that kitchen service (perhaps one could say even getting groceries) and cleaning duties alike are expected to be rotated on a regular basis. Likewise the concern for orderly handing over and maintenance of the tools necessary for these tasks, is not merely for the sake of order as a value in itself, but primarily for maintaining harmony and peace among the community.

Benedict's concern about a provost contending with the abbot stems from the principle that a community needs to have a clear leadership structure, headed by someone who cares for the community and looks after the needs of all. Two leaders on equal footing are bound at some point to cause division and conflict. Thus Benedict proposes that if a community is large enough to require a second leader at the helm, such a person should be appointed by the primary leader of the community (naturally in consultation with the whole community, as is advised in chapter 4 on community governance and decision making). To understand better how this might translate into a non-monastic Benedict Option community context, the respective roles of abbot and provost envisioned by St. Benedict are as follows:

Abbot/Abbess: full responsibility for the whole governance of the community; holds highest executive role within the community, and bound by obedience to care for the good of all, while having accountability to the community and to the external authorities of the church hierarchy; further delegates authority to others within the community responsible for specific aspects of community life. When the community also has a provost, the abbot frequently focuses on overall community structure and representing the community in relations with other entities outside the community, while the provost focusing on internal, day to day administration of the community.

Provost: second authority to the abbot, delegated by the abbot to share their responsibility of authority and governance of the community, often focusing on day to day administration of community operations.

11

DISCIPLINE AND CORRECTION

If someone becomes stubborn or disobedient or proud, or if he grumbles or in any way bucks against the holy Rule and defies the direction of his seniors, then he should be admonished privately twice by the seniors in accordance with our Lord's direction. If he still does not amend, he should be rebuked publicly in the presence of everyone. But if even then he does not reform, let him be excommunicated, provided that he understands the nature of this punishment.

The measure of excommunication or punishment given should be in proportion to the seriousness of a fault, which will be determined case by case by the abbot.

Those of every age and level of understanding should receive appropriate treatment.

If someone is found guilty of less serious faults, he should not be allowed to eat at the common table. Someone guilty of a more serious fault should be excluded from both the community meals and the community liturgies. Nobody in this case should associate or converse with him at all, and he should work alone at the tasks assigned to him.

However, the abbot must have the utmost care and concern for the offending brother, because it is not the healthy who need a physician, but the sick. Therefore, he should use every means a wise physician would use, and send to him ambassadors of the heart, that is, mature and wise members of the community who, privately, can go and console the wavering brother, urge him to humility as a way of making amends, and console him lest he be overwhelmed by excessive sorrow. Rather, as the Apostle also says: "Let love for him be reaffirmed," and let all pray for him.

The abbot must have the utmost solicitude to act with all discernment and diligence in order not to lose any of the sheep entrusted to him. He should realize that he has undertaken the care of the sick, not a tyranny over the healthy. He is to imitate the loving example of the Good Shepherd who left the ninety-nine sheep in the mountains and went in search of the one sheep that had strayed: "so great was his compassion for its weakness that he mercifully placed it on his sacred shoulders and so carried it back to the flock."

Anyone excommunicated for serious faults from the common prayer and from the table should make amends in this way: to prostrate himself in silence at the entrance of the chapel at the close of the Work of God. He should lie face down at the feet of all as they leave the chapel, and do this until the abbot judges that he has made satisfaction. Next, at the bidding of the abbot, let him prostrate himself at the abbot's feet, then at the feet of all that they may pray for him. Only then, if the abbot orders it, should he be admitted back to the common life in the rank the abbot assigns.

Those excommunicated for less serious faults only from the table should make amends in the chapel as above, but only for as long as the abbot deems appropriate. He should indicate this with his blessing and say: "It is enough."

If anyone makes a mistake singing a psalm, responsory, refrain or reading, he must perform some small act of satisfaction then and there before all. If he does not use this occasion to humble himself, he should be subjected to more severe punishment for failing to correct by humility the wrong he committed through negligence.

If someone commits a fault while at any work—working in the kitchen, in the storeroom, in serving, in the bakery, in the garden, in any craft or anywhere else—either by breaking or losing something or failing in some other way, he should at once come before the abbot and the community of his own accord and admit his fault and make satisfaction. If his fault is made known through another, he is to be subjected to a more severe correction. When the cause of his sin lies hidden in his conscience alone, however, he is to reveal it only to the abbot or to one of the spiritual elders who know how to heal their own wounds as well as those of others without exposing them and making them public.

If a brother has been corrected frequently for any fault, or if he has even been excommunicated, and yet does not amend, he should receive a stronger punishment. But if even then he does not reform, or perhaps becomes proud and would actually defend his conduct, which God forbid, the abbot should follow the method of a wise physician. After he has applied the bandage of persuasion, the ointment of encouragement, the medicine of divine Scripture, and finally the cauterizing iron of excommunication, and yet his earnest efforts are still unsuccessful, let him apply an even better remedy: the abbot and all the brothers should pray for the wayward brother so that the Lord, who can do all things, may bring about the health of the sick brother. Yet if even this procedure does not heal him, then finally, the abbot must expel him from the community entirely.

If someone, following his own evil ways, departs from the monastery but then wishes to return, he must first promise to make full amends for leaving. He may then be received back, but as a test of his humility he should be given the lowest rank. If he leaves again, or even a third time, he should be readmitted under the same conditions. After this third time, however, he must understand that he will be denied all prospect of return.

Commentary: *In a monastery itself, the practice of regulations and discipline is more like that in an individual family or household than like what we might be about as a community of families forming something together like a village or a town. Thus, the particular details will not apply in the same way in a typical BenOp community as they would in a monastery (indeed, it would be unjust to try and apply them strictly in the same way!). But, respecting the dignity and autonomy of the individual persons and families in the community, the core underlying principles regarding justice and equity can be brought to inform the rules and norms for any community or organization in a very beneficial way.*

This chapter should always be read in light of the following chapter on caring for the weak, for all the principles of discipline and correction are for the sake of caring for the weak. We are all of us wounded by sin, and incomplete in ourselves, needing norms and guidelines to help us live in harmony with one another for mutual support in growing unto union with Christ.

Note well that right at the beginning Benedict reiterates the Gospel principle of admonishing in private rather than public shaming, and that all correction and discipline for wrong-doing should be designed for the good of the person in question, and never merely to punish them. Benedict strongly emphasizes how a leader ought always to be oriented toward the care and solicitude for those entrusted to them, less like a tyrant and more like a wise physician.

While it may seem at first glance a bit harsh for Benedict to urge self-imposed corrective action for someone who makes a mistake during singing the psalms or during work, he has a very good reason for identifying these kinds of incidents. These points are insightful observations on how to preserve community peace and cohesion precisely in those small things that are so susceptible to irritate and become in time causes of hatred and strife.

12

CARING FOR THE WEAK

Care of the sick must be held above and before all else, so that they may be served truly as Christ himself, for he said: "I was sick and you visited me," and, "What you did for one of the least of these you did for me."

Let the sick on their part bear in mind that they are served out of honor for God, and let them not by their excessive demands distress their brothers who serve them. Still, they must be borne with patiently, because serving such as these merits a greater reward. Consequently, the abbot should take great care that they suffer no neglect.

The abbot must take the greatest care that cellarers and those who serve the sick do not neglect them, for the shortcomings of his subordinates are his responsibility.

Although human nature itself is inclined to be compassionate toward the old and the very young, the authority of the Rule should also provide for them. Since their weakness must always be taken into account, in no way should they be required to follow the strictness of the Rule with regard to food, but should be treated with tender consideration and allowed to eat before the appointed times.

Commentary: *The principle of adjusting expectations for the old, the young, and the infirm, especially as regards physical needs illustrates the value that the way of St. Benedict places on the love of Christ above all and the solicitude and care for helping all to reach Christ, not getting hung up on rigidity in regards to secondary things.*

13

FOOD, DRINK, AND SLEEP

The monks are to receive bedding as arranged by the abbot, suitable to monastic life. If possible, all are to sleep in one area, but if the size of the community precludes this, they should sleep in groups of ten or twenty under the watchful care of more senior monks. A candle should be kept burning in the room until morning. They should sleep clothed, and wearing their belts (but they should remove their knives, lest they accidentally cut themselves while sleeping). Thus the monks will always be ready to arise without delay when the signal is given; each will hasten to come to the Work of God with seriousness and composure.

The more adolescent should not have their beds next to each other, but interspersed among those of their seniors. On arising for the Work of God, they should quietly encourage one other, since grogginess makes them prone to excuses.

Everyone has his own gift from God, one this and another that. Therefore, it is not without some misgiving that we specify the amount of food and drink for others:

It is written: "distribution was made to each one as he had need." By this we do not imply that there should be favoritism – far from it – but rather consideration for weaknesses. Whoever needs less should thank God and not be saddened, but whoever needs more should be humbled by his weakness, and not self-important on account of such consideration.

In this way all the members will be at peace. Before all else, there must be no murmuring or grumbling for any reason whatsoever, whether in word or deed. If anyone is caught grumbling, they should undergo severe disciplinary action.

We believe it suffices for the daily meal, whether at noon or in mid-afternoon, to provide each table with two kinds of cooked food because of divers individual needs. In this way, someone who may not be able to eat one kind of food may partake of the other. Therefore, two dishes should suffice for all, and if fruit or fresh vegetables are available, a third may be added as well.

A pound of bread should be enough each day whether for only one meal or both dinner and supper. In the latter case the cellarer should set aside a third of the pound for serving with supper. Should it happen that the work is harder than usual, the abbot may decide to add a little something extra, as appropriate. Above all, they should avoid overindulgence, lest a monk get indigestion. Nothing is so contrary to the Christian way of life as overindulgence, as Our Lord affirms: "see to it that your hearts are not weighed down with overindulgence."

However, in view of the feebleness of the infirm, we believe that a half portion of wine per person is sufficient each day. But to those whom God gives the strength to abstain should know that they will have their own reward. The provost may decide that local conditions, work, or the summer heat demands a greater amount of drink, being solicitous to avoid excess and drunkenness.

We read that wine is not a drink for monks, but since in our days monks cannot be convinced of this, let us at least agree not to drink to excess, but moderately, for "wine makes even the wise go astray."

The abbot's table should always be for the guests and travelers. Whenever there are no guests, it is within the abbot's power to invite any of the brothers he wishes.

There should be a separate kitchen for the abbot and guests (who are never lacking in a monastery), that the brothers not be disturbed when guests arrive at odd hours.

Commentary: *Notice the key principle throughout all these eminently practical considerations is that every necessity should be provided for (as best as possible) so that no-one should have cause for grumbling, and that all might have the support to be free to pursue the calling articulated in the beginning: to open our eyes to the deifying light, keep our tongues from deceit, turn away from evil and do good, and seek and strive after the peace of Christ.*

Note well that everything regarding food and drink is mentioned very tentatively by Benedict, making no hard and fast rule for everybody, recognizing as he does that each person has their own particular needs, gifts and abilities. Obviously this principle applies also to more than just food, drink, and sleep. There is great wisdom here in adapting to the needs of varying circumstances as well, whether on account of seasonal variations, particularly strenuous labors, or even the particular dietary needs of different individuals.

At the end of it all, there is still a very practical eye to hospitality—in light of the inevitable intrusions of circumstance into the community's daily routines—and to maintaining the peaceful flow of life in the community.

14

TRAVEL

Those who work too far away and are unable return to the chapel at the appointed times – and the abbot determines that such is the case – should perform the Work of God where they are, bending their knee in reverence to the divine.

Likewise, those who are traveling are not to omit the established times for prayer, but to as much as possible to perform the prayers as best they can, taking care not to neglect to perform the divine service allotted to them.

If someone is sent anywhere expecting to return that same day to the monastery, they should not presume to eat while out, even if someone begs them to do so, unless their abbot prepared it beforehand.

If some monk traveling from distant provinces should come and wish to stay as a guest in the monastery, and they are content with the ways of the place as they find it, (and does not disrupt the monastery by superfluous demands, but is simply content with what they find), then they should be received for as long as they desire.

If they should reasonably catch or point out anything with the humility of love, then the abbot should wisely consider whether it may be for this very thing that the Lord has led them there.

If after a while the visiting monk wishes to make firm their stability, such a wish should not be refused, all the more so when there is time to be able to discern their life while they are a guest.

Commentary: *Throughout this chapter on the subject of travel, we can see very clearly that the Benedict Option way presupposes—indeed depends on—close geographical proximity of members of the community to one another around a central place and a very locally-oriented way of life.*

For those whose responsibilities take them beyond walking distance to the chapel, they must nonetheless not neglect the customary prayers at the appointed times. We can learn two things from this fact of particular relevance for living the Benedict Option: (1) the absolute centrality of prayer-as-formative-liturgy in the life and soul of the Christian in a non-Christian world, and (2) the expectation that these prayers (consisting mostly of the psalms) would be in fact memorized to a greater or lesser degree by most members of the community. There is much here that any Benedict Option community can learn from.

On the point of eating within the community only, and not taking food while outside the community setting, it is important to note that traditional societies almost universally recognize that to eat with someone is to enter into communion with them in some way, and places in you the position of adopting to some level their customs and religious practices. This is not to say by any stretch of the imagination that one should share meals only with members of the same community, but rather that we need to be aware of, and have respect for, the formative nature of meals and culinary practices. How are you forming your soul and the soul of your family and community with the way you practice meals and approach food?

Not only does the holy Benedict account for how those who follow in his way should relate to travel themselves, but he also gives account for how other travelers such as guests and visitors to the community are to be received and welcomed, in such a way as to not disrupt the community with superficiality—for the Lord often sends such travelers for a purpose. Getting to know someone in this way is also an excellent opportunity for both they and the community to mutually discern the possibility for a common way of life.

15

WORK AND ART

Ennui and the lack of direction is the enemy of the soul. Therefore, at set intervals the brothers should be occupied in manual labor, and also at set times in divine reading (*Lectio Divina*).

To achieve this goal, we believe that the times for both activities may be arranged as follows: From Pascha (Easter) to the first of October, in the early morning when they leave from praying the first hour until nearly the fourth hour they should labor at whatever needs to be done. From that hour until the midday prayer, they should be free to devote themselves to reading. But after midday prayer and having risen from table, they may rest in their beds in complete silence; or should anyone wish to read to themselves, let them do so, so long as they don't disturb the others. The ninth hour prayers should be said a little early—about middle of the eighth hour—and from then on they should work at whatever needs to be done until evening prayer.

From the first of October until the beginning of Lent, they should be free to devote themselves to reading until the end of the second hour. At this time the third hour prayers should be said, and then until the ninth hour all should labor at the work assigned to them. At the first signal for the ninth hour, they each should break from their work to be ready for the second signal to sound. After the meal they should be free to devote themselves to their reading or to the psalms. During the days of Lent, they should be free to devote themselves to their reading from early morning until the third hour, after which until the end of the tenth hour they should work at what has been assigned to them.

If the needs of the place or their poverty should force them to work at the harvesting themselves, they should not be saddened, for when they live by the labor of their own hands, then they are true monks, as was done by both our fathers and the apostles. Yet, all things should be done in a measured way on account of the fainthearted.

In all instances, help should be available when needed, so that all may serve without grumbling. On the other hand, when they have less work, they should go out to whatever work is assigned them.

Brothers who are sick or weak should be assigned some kind of work or craft that will neither make them idle nor overwhelm them or drive them away with excessive toil. The abbot must take their feebleness into account.

The care of the monastery's property, whether tools, clothing, or anything else, the abbot should entrust to those brothers whose life and character he is sure of. To them alone, as he shall judge useful, should be entrusted the things to be cared for and to be collected again. The abbot should keep a short list of these things, so that as the brothers take over for one another in their assignments, he may know what he gives and what he receives back.

If someone entrusted with the task treats the monastery's things in a sloppy or negligent way, they should be rebuked, and if they do not make amends, they should fall under the discipline of the rule.

If there are any artisans in the monastery, they should practice their craft with all humility, if the abbot permits. If one of them becomes puffed up in the knowledge and skill of their craft, because they seem to be conferring something on the monastery, they are to be removed from their craft and not go back to it unless, with humility the abbot orders them to take it up again.

If any work of these artisans are to be sold, those whose hands the transactions pass through should see to it that they not dare to practice any fraud. Let them always remember Ananias and Sapphira, who incurred bodily death, lest they and all who commit fraud in monastery affairs suffer death in their soul. The evil of greed must not creep in when setting the prices of these things, but rather the price should always be set a little lower than people living in the world are able to give, so that in all things God may be glorified.

Commentary: *Just as structured prayer and leisure have been given their place in the Benedictine way of life, so also work (broadly understood) is allotted its place. It is important to note that "work" in the Benedictine sense of the word does **not mean** activity for the sheer sake of keeping busy—no, that would be antithetical to authentic Christian life—but rather for the way of Benedict the goal is to avoid aimlessness and ennui (mindless distraction and boredom being the breeding ground for the soul-sickness known as **acedia**), and the Benedictine concept of "work" includes not only manual labor but also all manner of craftsmanship, and even proper study and reading.*

Just like with prayer, Benedict arranges respective times for work and study/reading that adjust with the change of sea-

sons, so as to make the best use of the time of day appropriate to what needs to be done during the different times of the year.

Although a community should eventually be able to sustain itself by its own work and produce, the Benedict Option ideal is not that you should have to grow all your own food (nor produce all your own goods) yourself. But if you do find in your circumstances that growing your own food is necessary, then you should do so with a grateful heart, keeping in mind all the while not to unduly overburden yourselves and lose sight of God's loving providence for us.

Related to work is the subject of the very tools and equipment we use for our work. Benedict advised that common property of the community should be entrusted to the care and supervision of trustworthy persons who will take good care of it and make sure it is used well and returned to their care in good condition by those who use it, for the common good to which it has been entrusted.

Craftsmen and artisans in the community are to perform their trade with humility, recognizing that their gifts and talents are from God for the service the community and the good of humanity, not merely a tool for their own profit or self-aggrandizement. The Benedict Option market economics basic principle #1 (summarizing the Gospel teachings on the matter) is: avoid fraud and any calculative concern for money, but rather set the price for any goods or services provided to be slightly less than what people can reasonably afford, **so that in all things God may be glorified**.

16

CHRIST IN OTHERS

All guests arriving are to be received as though they were Christ, for he himself will say: "I was a guest and you received me." All due honor should be shown to guests, especially to those of the household of the faith and to pilgrims.

As soon as a guest has been announced, the prior or the brothers are to meet them with all the service of charity. First of all, they should pray together and in this way be joined in the fellowship of peace, for the kiss of peace (signifying the official reception of the guest as brother or sister in Christ) should not be offered unless preceded by prayer, on account of the possibility of diabolical deceptions.

In every greeting to guests, humility is to be shown to all when arriving or departing, by bowing your head or by a full-body prostration, because it is Christ who is adored in them and received.

Being this received, the guests should be led into prayer; and then seated with the prior or with one who has been appointed for this. The divine law (i.e. the Gospel) should be read before the guest for their edification, and after this let gentleness and kindness be shown to them.

The prior may break his fast for the sake of a guest, unless it is one of the principal days of fasting that cannot be violated. The brothers, however, will follow the customary fast.

The abbot should give the guests water for their hands, and the abbot with those gathered should wash the feet of all the guests, after which they recite this verse: "We have received, O God, your mercy in the midst of your temple."

In receiving the poor and pilgrims, the greatest care and solicitude should be shown, because in them all the more is Christ received; as to the rich, the fear of them already commands them respect.

The care of the sick must before all and above all be adhered to, so that they may be served truly as Christ, for he himself has said: "I was sick and you visited me," and, "whatever you did for one of the least of these, you did for me."

Commentary: *Lest we become bogged down in the distractions of quotidian affairs of life, we are called back here to the centrality of Christ within Christian community. I cannot emphasize this enough: any Benedict Option community is an utter failure if it does not cultivate the authentic Christian charity of seeing others as Christ.*

Recognizing both the importance of receiving the other in Christ, and also the reality of temptation to turn away from Christ and be drawn away from prayer, Benedict guides us with this simple rule: Guests are to be received first of all with prayer and a blessing, in order to avoid the deceptions of the evil one using this as an opportunity to lead one or another astray. In this way we begin the encounter between guest and host as one embedded in the heart of God. It is worth noting that especially in such an anxiously weary and suspicious world as we inhabit today, it is of vital importance to cultivate this mysticism that Benedict outlines for us regarding Christ the guest.

The washing of the feet that Benedict mentions in this chapter has particular relevance in those societies where pilgrims spend days and weeks on end traveling on foot, and is thus a great kindness. Outside of such contexts, it is often more appropriate kindness to provide water for washing their hands, and making sure that they are otherwise comfortably provided for as the circumstances allow.

17

ORGANIZATIONAL ORDER

Do not easily grant entrance to those newly come to this way of life, but, as the Apostle affirms, "Test the spirit to see if it is from God."

Therefore, if they should persevere in knocking, and have put up with harsh treatment and the difficulty of entry after four or five days, and it is seen that they bear this patiently and persist in their petition, entry should be granted to them to be in the guest room for a few days.

After that, let them be in the novices' quarters, where they shall study and eat and sleep. A senior monk shall be assigned to them who is skilled at winning hearts, to watch over them with absolute diligence. He should take care to see whether they truly seek God: whether they are eager for the Work of God, and for obedience, and for humble and menial work.

The novice should be clearly told all the hardships and difficulties through which lies the way to God. If they promise perseverance in their stability, then after a period of two months this rule shall be read through to them, and they should be told, "Behold the law under which you wish to do battle. If you can observe, enter. If you really cannot, you are free to leave."

If they still would stand firm, they should be led back to the novices' quarters, and again thoroughly tested in all patience. After six months have gone by, the rule shall be read to them, so that they should know what is being entered into. If still they stand firm, then this same rule shall be reread to them once again after four months.

Then, if having deliberated within themselves, they promise to keep it in its entirety and to carry out every command enjoined on them, then they should be received into the community, knowing that the law of the rule establishes that from that day forward they shall not be allowed to leave from the monastery, nor to remove their neck from under the yoke of the Rule that they had been free to reject or accept under such a long period of deliberation.

When they are to be received, in the place for prayer, they shall in front of everyone promise their stability, their monastic way of life, and their obedience, before God and his saints, that if they ever do otherwise, they shall know that they will be condemned by the one whom they mock.

After the novice has placed the signed document of their written promise upon the altar, the novice himself should promptly intone this verse: "Receive me, O Lord, according to your promise and I will live, and let me never be confounded in my hope." The whole community is to reply three times with the same verse, adding "Glory be to the Father, and to the Son, and to the Holy Spirit." Then this novice shall prostrate themselves at the feet of each one of them that they might pray for them, and thenceforth from that very day they will be counted as one of the community.

They are to retain their rank in the monastery according to their time of entry into the monastic way of life, as distinguished by the merit of their lives, and also as the abbot places them.

Now the abbot must not disturb the flock entrusted to him nor, as though enjoying arbitrary power, arrange anything unjustly. He must always consider thoroughly that he will have to render to God an account of all his judgments and deeds.

And in no place whatever is age to determine rank, nor be prejudicial to it, for Samuel and Daniel as mere children judged their elders. Therefore, apart from those as mentioned above whom for some overriding consideration the abbot has promoted or demoted for certain reasons, all the rest should retain their rank according to their time of entry. So, for example, one who comes to the monastery in the second hour of the day must recognize that they are junior to someone who came in the first hour of the day, regardless of age or other distinction.

The juniors in the monastic way of life, then, ought to respect those who are more advanced than them, and the more advanced ought to love those more recently arrived. When they address one another by name, none should be allowed to call each another by their name alone; rather, the more advanced are to call their juniors "Brother," and the juniors are to call those more advanced than them "*Nonnus,*" which means "Revered Father."

But the abbot, because he is believed to act in the place of Christ, is to be called "Lord" and "Abba," not for any pretension of his own, but out of honor and love for Christ. He, for his part, should reflect on this, and should show himself to be worthy of such honor.

Wherever brothers meet one another, the junior one should ask the more advanced for a blessing. When an more advanced monk passes by, the less advanced one should rise and give them a place to sit, nor should the junior presume to sit down with them unless the senior bid them to do so, that in this way it shall be done as it is written: "They anticipate one another in showing honor to each other."

Commentary: *As anyone with experience in a community or organization knows, healthy ordering of the community structure—from first joining the community to navigating leadership and governance of the community—is vital for harmonious cohesion and maintaining peace and stability, not to mention Christian love and charity.*

As we know from long experience, not everybody wants to join this way of life for the same reasons, and sometimes for less than pure motives. Thus in any Benedict Option community newcomers and established residents should get to know one another first. Like many things in the Rule of St. Benedict, the particulars of novitiate life in a monastery are simply not applicable to most Benedict Option communities. However, the principles for discernment that Benedict identifies here have eminently practical relevance to our purposes. One observation in particular is helpful here, and that is the explicit laying out of clear expectations both on the part of the community and of the would-be applicant.

The three-fold commitment Benedict requests new members to make is to promise...

*1. **Stability:** reliability and putting down roots in the place,*

*2. **Obedience:** mutual obedience among members of the community, i.e. commitment to one another in the common service of Christ, under obedience to the Gospel, in obedience to God, and*

*3. **The Pattern of Life:** The promise to undertake for themselves this particular way of life (**conversatio**, or **schema**, as it is called in the East), as a way to pursue holiness in community with others.*

*Pay attention to the fact that the new member is making a self-oblation to **God** in this act, and **not** to the community itself nor any member or leader thereof. In ordinary BenOp communities this commitment may be more or less formal, seeing as individuals and families living in the world are not binding themselves to strict monastic life in such a case, but only by analogy imitating the spirit of monastic oblation in their personal commitment to a shared way of life in this or that particular community.*

In any decision of governance, Benedict Option leadership must arrange all things for the good of each of the community members, and not merely the good of one or another individual or class alone.

Again, the particular titles of respect developed in specifically monastic culture may not be completely applicable in a typical Benedict Option context, but the principle of honor and respect, of love and care, should be a guiding light in developing an organic and harmonious structure of community organization.

On a related note, it used to be the custom—and still is where such cultures are nurtured—in traditionally Christian cultures for people to give blessings to one another, whatever their state in life, and not reserved only to clergy. Thus a mother or a father blesses their children, or a schoolteacher might bless their students, or an elderly member of the village might offer his or her blessing to the young man or woman who greats them in the piazza as they pass by. Certainly the blessings of clergy are particular and have a more solemn or specialized character for certain occasions, but we should not thereby neglect the practice of the more quotidian blessings that strengthen us in Christ through the daily hardships of life. Every Christian in virtue of his or her baptism is called to be a blessing and to bless.

18

PROMOTION TO LEADERSHIP

In appointing an abbot, this line of reason should always be considered: that the person selected should be the one chosen by the unanimous decision of the whole community according the fear of God, or else elected by whatever small part of the community possesses sounder judgment.

The one to be appointed abbot should be elected because of the merit of their life and the wisdom of their teaching, even if they are in the lowest rank in the community.

But if the whole community should conspire to elect someone who will consent to their vices—may such a thing never happen—and this somehow becomes known to the bishop in whose diocese this takes place, or to the other abbots or for that matter to any of the Christians in the vicinity, they should prevent this conspiracy of the wicked from gaining the upper hand, and instead appoint a worthy steward over this house of God. They should know that they will receive a good reward for this, if done with purity of intention and zeal for God, just as they will fall into sin if they neglect to do so.

Once in office, the abbot must always keep in mind what kind of burden they have taken on, and to whom they will have to render an account of their stewardship. The abbot should also understand that it is better to serve others than to rule over them.

The abbot, therefore, ought to be well-versed in the divine law, so that they may "know a place from which to bring forth old treasures and new."

The abbot must be pure, sober, and merciful, and always should exalt mercy over judgment, so that the same may be done for them.

The abbot should hate the vices, but love the brothers. In dealing out correction, the abbot should do so prudently and not go too far; lest, by scraping too hard to remove the rust, the vase itself should shatter. His own fragility, the abbot should have always before his eyes, and be mindful "that the bruised reed must not be broken." By this we're not saying that they should allow vices to sprout and grow, but rather to prune them away prudently and with charity in whatever way looks best as we have already said, and strive more to be loved than feared.

The abbot should not be agitated and anxious, nor excessive and obstinate, nor jealous and overly suspicious, for such a person never will be at rest. Instead, the abbot should be considerate and provident in his commands, and whether the work he assigns pertains to God or to the world, the abbot should be discerning and balanced, reflecting upon the discretion of holy Jacob, saying: "If I drive my flocks too hard in one day, they will all die." Therefore, drawing on this and other examples of discretion—the mother of the virtues, the abbot should manage all things so that the strong have something to yearn for and the weak nothing to run from.

Commentary: *Whenever human beings come together to organize themselves around a common way of life, or any shared endeavor, there will need to be those who assume responsibility for leading and ordering all things well. And so it has been ordained from the beginning of creation, for man is made to be the image and likeness of God the King of the Universe. The two equally pernicious errors we must avoid in our human organization of leadership are tyrannical despotism and fatally leveling egalitarianism—both errors will destroy any authentic Christian community. Rather, to the one who would lead Christ says, "you must be the servant of all," and also that you must "take up your cross and follow me" who am the True King and so lead my people in imitation of the Good Shepherd.*

Note that the abbot is elected from among those capable of exercising authority, and Benedict allows for the option of either unanimous (i.e. consensus decision rather than a majority-vote model) election by the entire community, or for unanimous election by a smaller group of the community who are known to possess greater wisdom. This is to help avoid the problems associated with mob-rule or populism in its various forms, that arise from time to time in the life-cycles of human society. The leader of a Benedictine community is always accountable to a higher authority, and Benedict himself also outlines the norms and obligations in this chapter for the correction of abuses of office.

The criteria for choosing the leader are: their virtuous character—the worthiness of their way of life—and the wisdom of their teaching. It doesn't matter otherwise what rank they hold, or background credentials they have. Note also that from the beginning of the Benedictine way it has been known that **men and women are both equally capable of leadership over the Christian community**—*Benedict's own sister, Scholastica, was leader of a monastery of women—and traditional Christian practice reflects this (prior to the distortions of the roles of men and women that emerged in the early modern era). The leader must have the following qualities:*

- *A servant who is aware of the immense burden of leadership in the Christian community*
- *Well-versed in the Scriptures and wise in their application*

- *Watchful, awake, merciful, and single-heartedly devoted to God*
- *Like a doctor, healing without causing harm to the weak*
- *Interior stability and peaceful confidence*
- *Above all, discretion—i.e. the wise application to particular circumstances with foresight of what leads to the good of each.*

At the heart of it, what is required is humility and magnanimity—greatness of spirit—on the part of both the community and its leaders: The community needs to have the humility to recognize its need for authentic leadership in order to be organized well and the leaders need the humility and self-knowledge to serve the community as Christ, the community needs the magnanimity to strive for greatness and set high expectations and the leaders need the magnanimity to lead the community in Christ by taking up their own cross of seeking the good of all those entrusted to them.

19

GREATNESS AND SERVICE

Just as there is an evil zeal of bitterness which separates from God and leads to hell, so also there is a good zeal which separates from wrongdoing and leads to God and into everlasting life.

This, then, is the good zeal which monks should exercise with a most burning love: "to outdo one another in showing honor to one another," and with the greatest patience putting up with each other's weaknesses whether of body or of character, and strive to surpass one another in mutual obedience.

No one is to pursue what is useful only for himself, but what is of greater service for another, and so they should show pure brotherly love.

They should fear God with love. They should love their abbot with a sincere and humble love. They should prefer nothing whatsoever to Christ, that He may lead us all in like manner into eternal life.

The reason we have written this rule is that, by observing it in monasteries, we can show how to obtain at least some degree of moral uprightness, or at least the beginnings of this way of life. But for anyone hastening on to the perfection of this way of life, there are the teachings of the holy Fathers of the Church, the observance of which may lead a person to the very heights of perfection.

In fact, what page—what word, even—of the divine author of the Old and New Testaments does not contain the truest norms for human life? What book of the holy catholic fathers does not resonate as drawing us along the right course to to our Creator? Or what of the Conferences and the Institutes of the Fathers, or their lives, and even the rule of our holy father Basil? What else are they but the instruments of virtue of exemplary and obedient monks?

You, therefore, who are hastening toward the heavenly homeland, with the help of Christ fulfill this minimal rule for beginners. Then at length, as we've mentioned above, you will come to the greater heights of teaching and virtue under God's protection. Amen.

Commentary: *Benedict here contrasts the two kinds of zeal that can exist in the human heart: the zeal of bitterness and jealousy that separates us from God, and the good zeal that energizes us to resist every vice and unites us in love to God. This latter is what gives us the power to strive unceasingly to pursue holiness not only for own sakes but also for the good of our brothers and sisters in Christ. This zeal within a community should lead us to outdo one another in honoring one another, with love and patience supporting each other in our Christian life. This is the very power behind our coming together into living Christian communities—to seek holiness together and collaborate in cultivating a way of life wherein our Christian vocation to holiness and divinization becomes not only possible, but even as natural as breathing. So may it be always.*

Above all, such zeal should keep us focused on keeping first things first and second things second, in their proper order of goods, so that we should put nothing whatsoever ahead of Christ, but rather putting Christ himself before—and at the core of—everything else. This is true discernment.

Benedict closes by reminding us that the Rule is the foundation for Christian living-well and a guide for beginners in forming Christian community and seeking to put into practice authentically the Benedict Option. From here we can build upon this basic beginning and advance in true Christian life, through the teachings of the holy fathers of the Church (especially John Cassian and Basil the Great) and Sacred Scripture, so that we might form not only Christian communities but even become true communities of sanctity.

So may we all, by following this minimum guide for beginning the Benedict Option and supporting one another in living the Christian way of life, arrive together at the perfection of Christ who with the Father and the Holy Spirit be all honor and glory now and unto the ages of ages. Amen.

Appendix 1

Two Supporting Essays

By

Dr. Cameron M. Thompson

CHRISTIAN CULTURE: WHY BOTHER?

"God did not deign to save man by means of a mere syllogism..." (St. John Henry Newman) but rather He became Incarnate and lived among us, thus giving us not only knowledge and command- ment, but a way of life.

Why bother with Christian culture? Isn't being a good Christian simply a matter of doctrine and morals, follow- ing certain rules and believing certain things—a mere mat- ter of faith?

First we should ask: what do we mean by culture? Well, the word 'culture' comes from the Latin word *cultus*, which means worship or, if you will, ritual action. It is also relat- ed to the idea of cultivation, as in *agriculture* (care and tend- ing of the fields), *viticulture* (care and tending of the vines), or *horticulture* (care and tending of gardens), and so on. So perhaps one could say that *cultus* (the root of culture), as the systems of ritual and worship, has conceptually a sense to it of "care and tending of divine things."

Christopher Dawson, that preeminent scholar of Chris- tian history, defines culture as "the more or less stable, if continually developing, practices, norms, institutions, and relationship systems of a people, that endures from gener- ation to generation." In other words, culture is a relatively stable, if evolving, thing—that encompasses the whole network or complex system of social practices, institutions, and norms, which which have at their center the care and tending of divine things, or gods—whatever those gods may be. I might add that culture is typically not something that is done self-consciously, but rather something "done" (or rather, participated in) almost semi-consciously or nat- urally—in the same way breathing is done mostly without thought. Just like you've been doing right now, up to this moment. Except now you've become aware of your breathing because I've just pointed it out to you. Perhaps in becoming aware of your breathing you've noticed something about it, whether it is fast or slow, shallow or deep. In this same way, we often go about participating in the culture around us without noticing (1) *that* we're doing it, nor (2) *what* the particular qualities of the cultural rituals are that we're participating in. That is, just what *are* the divine things—or gods—that my actions, relationships, and institutions center on: Christ or the gods of Babylon?

So from all this we might say that a specifically Christian culture is one wherein it is natural—as natural as breathing—for one's life to be oriented to the divine things of Christ at the center of *all* social practices, norms, institutions, and relationships. This is not the same as saying that this orientation is self-conscious—but rather that the ebb and flow of participation in the ritual systems and practices of Christ's Incarnate power in the world is as natural as breathing.

So that's what a Christian culture *is*, but that brings us to the question of why should we bother with Christian culture at all? So what? Surely it is all very interesting, all very well and good for a historical study, but culture doesn't guarantee sanctity after all, and isn't the goal of Christian life really just to have faith, or a personal relationship with Christ? Now, the word 'faith' (and its related concept, 'belief') is an interesting thing. In the post-secular society we in the Modern Global West inhabit, we tend to think that faith (and belief) means assenting in some way or another to a set of propositions, or for the more cynical, "faith means believing what I know ain't true" (Mark Twain); however, this is not what the word faith (and belief) actually, or historically, means. Period. This popular (mis)conception of the term actually refers to mere notional assent—the kind of knowledge about some fact or another that you've been told or found out yourself to be the case, but that's not biblical meaning of the word 'faith'.

The true concept of faith, which in the Greek of the Bible is *pistis* (and the verb 'to believe' is *pistevo*), which is what we in English might call 'religious belief', has less to do with notional assent assent to some *proposition*, so much as with loyalty to a *person*. The traditional concept of 'faith' has to do with what even in modern English we retain in the concept of *faithfulness* and *fidelity* (rooted in the word 'faith'/'fides'). We all acknowledge that the concept of faithfulness doesn't mean that he or she has many or particularly strong propositional beliefs (in, say, the quadratic equation, or that the Earth revolves around the sun), but rather that he or she is trustworthy and loyal to some person, and this fidelity is an ever-present life reality.

Taken then to the idea of Christian Faith, this means that Faith is not a matter of belief-knowledge, but a matter of trustworthy loyalty—one's trust *in* Christ, and also one's trustworthy loyalty *to* Christ in all aspects of one's life (for instance, in the enduring social practices, norms, institutions, and relationships one participates in with the formalness and organic nonchalance with which one breathes).

Thus a Christian culture is one wherein it is easier—or at least more natural—to concretely live out one's Christian faith: that is, one's fidelity to Christ and the social practices and structures that are the lived practice of one's trust in Him. It behooves us then to stop and examine the qualities of the social norms, practices, and institutions we so naturally and unconsciously are participating in, and to find out just what are the "divine things"—or gods—that are at their center. And in order to better understand how we might rectify our situation, should we find ourselves embedded in a cultural system that is at odds with fidelity to, and trust in, Christ as Lord, then it will be necessary for us to re-cultivate through communities a living and authentic Christian culture. For, a Christian culture is the fertile soil of a Christian life, and without it, all the doctrine and law and moralizing in the world is the merest pretense of a withering branch, whose only hope for roots—let alone for bearing abiding fruit—is to be re-embedded into the soil of a living Christian community. Sure, Christian culture isn't a guarantee you'll be a saint, but it may just be a necessary precondition, at least for most of us humans of flesh and blood.

So why bother? Simply put, a Christian culture is a culture wherein it is possible—perhaps the only way possible—to live a Christian life and become holy.

WHAT WE CAN LEARN
FROM THE MONASTERY

When I graduated from college, I spent the summers working grounds-keeping at a rural monastery. In addition to what one might expect to learn about prayer and such at a monastery, one thing in particular took me by surprise. One of my jobs was to clean and re-stain the aging wood siding of the hermitages. Now, I should explain the physical arrangement of the monastery: lining the central garden each monk has a private hermitage (small 1-room cabin) where he sleeps and spends time in private prayer. In front of each hermitage is a small private garden (about 10' x 10') that the monk maintains and designs as he wishes.

As I was in these private gardens day after day while re-staining the siding of the hermits' individual cabins, I began to notice little details in their gardens that would otherwise escape notice. Some were symmetrical, others had mis-matched patches of herbs, many had a cherry tree in the center, and one even was starting to grow grape vines. The order and beauty (some of them rather more wild than tame) of these little plots really began to make an impression on me. One day I realized that each of these hermitage gardens was in its own way the monk's personal plot of paradise on earth for which he was responsible. These little gardens fulfilled each monk's God-given desire and command to bring order and peace to the earth. Even though he will never leave this monastery, he is bettering the Earth in the small way apportioned to him.

This consideration led me to realize that the same applies to all of us, albeit in a less obvious way. We each have a small little bit of earth (house, apartment, dorm room, or community garden) that we are responsible to bring peace and order to. By improving this little bit of turf we have into a tiny paradise, each of us, in our own small way, is increasing peace and order in the world as a whole.

This applies not only to the ground we plant and maintain, but also to our very selves. The monks understand this in their own lives. They've dedicated their lives to contemplative prayer so that by uniting themselves to God, they more deeply unite all humanity to God. Each of them—each of us as a human person—stands in the place of all humanity. We are all connected in our humanity. When one of us is filled with malice and sin, all humanity suffers. When one of us prays and receives the Love of God, all of humanity is drawn into that encounter with the Divine.

Appendix 2

The Ladder of Humility: In sequence according to practical development.

By

Dr. Cameron M. Thompson

THE LADDER OF HUMILITY: PRACTICAL STEPS

The following is the proper sequential ordering of the steps or degrees of the ladder of humility discussed in chapter 8. The steps ("rungs of the ladder") have been translated into practical actions to be taken, in sequential order, to acquire, though authentic humility, that perfect love that unites us to Christ.

1. **The first step:** Overcome distractedness and forgetfulness by becoming mindful of the world around you, engaging fully in the present moment, attentive to the task at hand. In this present moment, you already stand before the face of God in all that you do.

2. **The second step:** Practice communicating with others clearly, gently, and attentively. Thus overcome the uncharitable avoidance of truly encountering others. Develop the skills to speak well and articulately.

3. **The third step:** Say what you mean and mean what you say. That is, overcome the anxiety of cynicism, sarcasm, and jokesterism. Often times we hide behind humor or sarcasm as masks in order to avoid engaging our true selves with others. Practice sincerity and genuineness with others.

4. **The fourth step:** Practice sitting in silence, and overcome the anxiety of needing constant noise and stimulation. Become comfortable in silence, both exterior and interior silence.

5. **The fifth step:** Overcome the anxiety of self-determinism and neomania, by following the tried and true ways for accomplishing what must be done. Practice following the example and advice of exemplars of human excellence, and be about what you're about.

6. **The sixth step:** Overcome egocentrism and anxious self-preservation and practice the vulnerability of considering yourself more dispensable than others. This allows you to develop the habit of risking much for the good of others, and to not mistake the importance of the task or office for your own self-importance.

7. **The seventh step:** Let go of proud self-determination and practice being content in all circumstances, especially lack of resources or poor conditions. Develop the habit of remaining at peace and able to carry out your mission no matter what the situation.

8. **The eighth step:** Practice vulnerability and responsible transparency by becoming aware of your innermost thoughts and motivations. This is a work of both self-awareness and profound self-acceptance, and will allow you to begin to master yourself and enter more fully into relationships with others and the world around you.

9. **The ninth step:** Overcome obstinacy and the desire for control, and practice patience and perseverance in carrying out your mission. Do not shrink from difficulties or shirk responsibility in the face of difficulties

10. **The tenth step:** Practice obedience to your mission and to legitimate authority, and overcome rebelliousness and the anxiety of self-determinism.

11. **The eleventh step:** Overcome your whims, and practice embracing the will of God in all things.

12. **The twelfth step:** Practice attentive awareness to the presence of God, and develop the habit of remaining in awe and reverence. Flee from forgetfulness of His presence, and so overcome the fear of anything that is less than God. In this way you can become wholeheartedly dedicated to your mission.

Appendix 3

Schedule of Prayer

A Chart Illustrating the Times of
Daily Prayer Referred to in Chapter 9

DAILY TIMES FOR PRAYER
(LITURGY OF THE HOURS)

*"Seven times a day I have praised you,
and at midnight I arose to proclaim you."*

Morning Prayers: Morning worship service of psalms and prayers of praise around the time of sunrise.

First Hour of the Day: Shorter period of prayer around 6am, or immediately following Morning Prayers during the season when the sun rises later.

Third Hour: Brief prayer of the psalms at 9am or 10am, depending on the season.

Midday Prayers: Brief prayer of the psalms at 12pm.

Ninth Hour: Brief prayer of the psalms set to end around 3pm.

Evening Prayers: Evening worship service of psalms and prayers around the time of sunset, corresponding to the offering of incense in the temple of the Old Covenant.

Day's End Prayers: Nighttime worship service of psalms to complete the day around 9pm, orienting us to our final end.

Midnight Prayers: Approximately the middle of the night, consisting of psalms and readings from the Old Testament, sometimes shorter and sometimes longer, depending by season on the length of the night.

**Such are the times of prayer as Benedict envisions them, according to the practices common in his time. In practice, there evolved in various epochs and in different places variations in the length and precise placement of these prayers within the course of the day.